Contents

Meet the frogs

This tree frog spends most of its life in trees.

There are many different kinds of frogs all over the world. This frog is a tree frog. It lives in trees. The reed frog lives in **swamps**. All frogs live near water.

1 day

1 week

2 weeks

5 weeks

Frogs are amphibians.

All frogs are amphibians. An amphibian is an animal that spends part of its life in water and part of its life on land. In this book, you will find out about a common frog.

12 weeks

14 weeks

6–12 months

2 years

A mass of eggs

eggs

These frogs have laid their eggs in water.

All frogs begin life as tiny eggs. The tiny eggs are laid in the water. The eggs have to be kept wet all the time. These frogs have just laid masses of eggs in the water.

1 day

1 week

2 weeks

5 weeks

This mass of eggs is called spawn.

The mass of eggs is called **spawn**. Spawn looks like a big blob of jelly with little black dots in it. Each black dot inside an egg is a tiny tadpole.

The jelly supports the eggs and keeps them warm.

7

12 weeks

14 weeks

6–12 months

2 years

Hatching

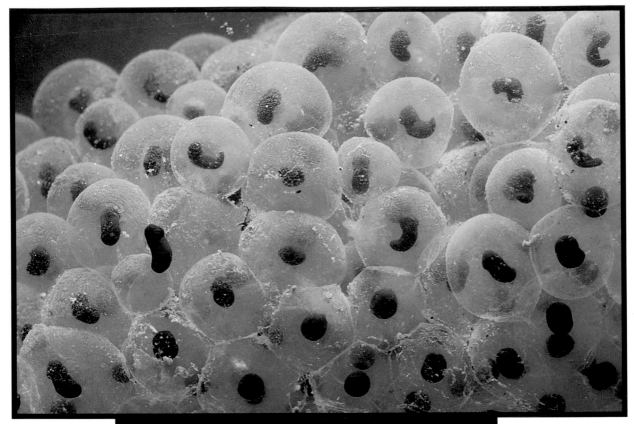

Can you see the tadpoles inside the eggs?

Some of the **spawn** is eaten by other animals and fish. But hundreds of eggs still survive. The tadpoles get bigger and bigger inside the eggs.

1 day

1 week

2 weeks

5 weeks

The tadpoles cling onto the spawn when they first hatch out of their eggs.

After about a week the tadpoles are ready to **hatch**. They push their way out of the eggs. But they do not move away from the spawn just yet. The tadpoles hang onto the spawn until their tails are longer and stronger.

12 weeks

14 weeks

6–12 months

2 years

gills

This tadpole has feathery gills to help it breathe under water.

Can you see the feathery **gills** on this tadpole?
Gills help a tadpole to breathe under water.
The gills take in **oxygen** from the water. Soon
the feathery gills will disappear.

1 day

1 week

2 weeks

5 weeks

This insect has caught a tadpole.

insect

tadpole

Some tadpoles are eaten by water insects or other animals. But many tadpoles do survive. They eat tiny plants and bits of pondweed. The tadpoles grow bigger and stronger.

12 weeks

14 weeks

6–12 months

2 years

5 weeks

This tadpole now has back legs.

back leg

When the tadpole is five weeks old, she starts to change into a frog. The back legs grow first.

1 day

1 week

2 weeks

5 weeks

mouth

surface

This tadpole has lungs so she can breathe at the water's surface.

After the back legs have grown the tadpole starts to grow **lungs** inside her body. Now that the tadpole has lungs she can go up to the surface of the pond to breathe air.

13

12 weeks

14 weeks

6–12 months

2 years

5–12 weeks

gill pouches

This tadpole's gill pouches are bulging. Soon her legs will push through them.

When the tadpole is between five and twelve weeks old her front legs start to appear. The front legs grow inside the tadpole's **gill** pouches.

1 day

1 week

2 weeks

5 weeks

This tadpole likes to catch water fleas in her wide mouth.

water fleas

At nearly twelve weeks the tadpole still needs her tail to help her swim among the plants. Now the tadpole likes to eat water fleas and other small insects instead of bits of pondweed.

15

12 weeks

14 weeks

6–12 months

2 years

12 weeks

webbed feet

This froglet's tail is shrinking.

At twelve weeks the tadpole is nearly a froglet!
Her tail starts to shrink. The froglet can swim
by pushing back her long back legs and
webbed feet.

 1 day

1 week

 2 weeks

 5 weeks

A frog only leaves the water when its tail has completely gone.

This tiny froglet has no tail now.

By fourteen weeks her tail has disappeared. The froglet climbs out of the water onto a leaf. She looks around and listens for signs of danger.

12 weeks

14 weeks

6–12 months

2 years

3 months

These froglets are all ready to leave the pond.

By three months the froglets are ready to leave the pond. They scramble onto lily plants and onto the bank. They hide under leaves and stones.

1 day

1 week

2 weeks

5 weeks

This froglet dives back into the pond to keep her skin wet.

A froglet's skin is very thin. It is important that it does not dry out. This froglet dives back into the pond to get wet again.

12 weeks

14 weeks

6–12 months

2 years

3–6 months

This frog catches an insect with her sticky tongue.

The frog is hungry. She sits very still and waits. An insect flies close by. The frog quickly flicks out her long, sticky tongue and catches the insect.

1 day

1 week

2 weeks

5 weeks

This grass snake is hunting for a frog to eat.

Grass snakes like to eat frogs. This grass snake is slithering towards the frog. The frog hears it. She dives into the pond to escape from the snake.

12 weeks

14 weeks

6–12 months

2 years

6–12 months

This frog has found a safe place to hibernate.

By autumn the frog is much bigger. She stores fat in her body. She lives off this fat when she **hibernates** for the winter. As winter comes the frog looks for a safe hole. She will stay here to hibernate.

1 day

1 week

2 weeks

5 weeks

This frog leaps off to find food.

The frog wakes up in the spring when the weather gets warmer. The frog has used up her store of fat and is hungry. Now she must leap off to find food.

12 weeks

14 weeks

6–12 months

2 years

2 years

Another year has passed and the frog is two years old. Her body is fat with eggs. The male frogs call to the female from the pond.

Male frogs call the female frogs by croaking loudly.

This female frog can hear the male frogs calling.

1 day

1 week

2 weeks

5 weeks

The male frog holds on to the female and they **mate**. After a while the eggs leave the female frog's body. A new mass of **spawn** floats away.

spawn

The male frog mates with the female frog.

12 weeks

14 weeks

6–12 months

2 years

Pond life

An adult frog's life is dangerous. Birds, fish and many animals not only feed on **spawn** and tadpoles, they also feed on adult frogs! If a frog is lucky and keeps out of danger, it can live for up to ten years.

This bird waits by the pond to see what it can catch to eat.

1 day

1 week

2 weeks

5 weeks

Frogs return to the pond every spring to lay eggs.

Every spring adult frogs return to the pond where they were born. They return to the pond to lay thousands of new eggs.

12 weeks

14 weeks

6–12 months

2 years

Life cycle

Frogspawn

Eggs hatching

2 weeks

5 weeks

12 weeks

5 months

1 year

2 years

Fact file

A frog can jump over three metres, so it could jump from the foot of your bed to right over your head!

Frogs can breathe through their skins as well as through their mouths.

When a frog first leaves the water it is about the same size as your thumb nail.

The largest frog is the goliath. It lives in Africa. It is large enough to eat small birds and mice.

The smallest frog in the world can be found in Cuba.

Glossary

gills   part of the body used to breathe in water

hatch   to come out of an egg

hibernate   to rest or sleep all winter

lungs   part of the body used to breathe in air

mate   a male and female come together to produce young

oxygen   a gas which living things need to breathe into their bodies to stay alive

spawn   a mass of eggs surrounded by jelly

swamp   wet, marshy ground

webbed feet   feet which have a layer of skin stretched between the toes

Index

Take-Off!

Life cycle of a
FROG

Angela Royston

Heinemann
LIBRARY

First published in Great Britain by Heinemann Library
Halley Court, Jordan Hill, Oxford OX2 8EJ
a division of Reed Educational and Professional Publishing Ltd
Heinemann is a registered trademark of Reed Educational and Professional Publishing Limited.

OXFORD   MELBOURNE   AUCKLAND
IBADAN   BLANTYRE   JOHANNESBURG   GABORONE
PORTSMOUTH NH   CHICAGO

Designed by Celia Floyd
Illustrations by Alan Fraser
Originated by Dot Gradations, UK
Printed in Hong Kong/China

04 03 02 01 00
10 9 8 7 6 5 4 3 2 1

ISBN 0 431 08406 8
This book is also available in hardback (ISBN 0 431 08401 7)

British Library Cataloguing in Publication Data

Royston, Angela
  Life cycle of a frog. – (Take-off!)
  1.Frogs – Life cycles - Juvenile literature
  I.Title II.Frog
  597.8'9

Acknowledgements

The Publisher would like to thank the following for permission to reproduce photographs:
Bruce Coleman Ltd/Hans Reinhard p21; Bruce Coleman Ltd/Jane Burton p14; Bruce Coleman Ltd/Kim Taylor pp20, 23; Bruce Coleman Ltd/William S Paton p22; Natural Science Photos/O C Roura p13; Natural Science Photos/Richard Revels pp6, 11; Natural Science Photos/Ward p.18; NHPA/David Woodfall p27; NHPA/G I Bernard p15; NHPA/Melvin Grey p26; NHPA/Stephen Dalton p4; OSF pp5, 10; OSF/David Thompson p9; OSF/G I Bernard pp7, 16, 24; OSF/Paul Franklin pp8, 12, 17; OSF/Stephen Dalton p19; OSF/Terry Heathcote p25.
Cover photograph: Oxford Scientific Films/Ian West

Our thanks to Sue Graves for her advice and expertise in the preparation of this book.

For more information about Heinemann Library books, or to order, please telephone +44(0)1865 888066, or send a fax to +44(0)1865 314091. You can visit our website at www.heinemann.co.uk

Any words appearing in bold, **like this**, are explained in the Glossary.